Please check all items for damages
before leaving the Library.
Thereafter you will be held
responsible for all injuries
to items beyond reasonable wear.

AUG   2003

GOLF

A TRUE BOOK®
by
Christin Ditchfield

Children's Press®
A Division of Scholastic Inc.

New York Toronto London Auckland Sydney
Mexico City New Delhi Hong Kong
Danbury, Connecticut

A young golfer
"chipping" the
ball to the green

Reading Consultant
Nanci R. Vargus, Ed.D.
Assistant Professor
Literacy Education
University of Indianapolis
Indianapolis, IN

Library of Congress Cataloging-in-Publication Data

Ditchfield, Christin.
  Golf / by Christin Ditchfield.
    48 p. cm. — (A true book)
    Summary: Examines the history, basic rules, terminology, and major
  events of the sport of golf.
  Includes bibliographical references and index.
    ISBN 0-516-22590-1 (lib. bdg.)   0-516-26961-5 (pbk.)
    1. Golf—Juvenile literature. [1. Golf.] I. Title. II. Series.
  GV968 .D58 2003
  796.352—dc21

                                                              2002005896

Contents

Tiger Woods
competing in
the Masters golf
tournament
in 1997

Tigermania

In 1997, millions of television viewers tuned in to watch the Masters—the most respected **tournament** in professional golf. Everyone wanted to see a young player named Tiger Woods.

Golf experts said that Tiger had an amazing gift for the

sport. His swing was smooth. His shots were accurate. He stayed calm under pressure. Tiger had all the skills he needed to challenge the best players in the world—and he was only 21 years old.

Tiger had been a professional player for less than a year. This was his first time competing in the Masters. During those four days, Tiger treated the fans to a fantastic display of championship golf.

Tiger Woods amazed fans with his record-breaking victory at the Masters in 1997.

He shot a combined score of 270 to win the tournament by 12 strokes. He was the youngest player ever to win the Masters.

Tiger Woods talking to the press

Tiger's victory at the Masters made him an instant **celebrity**. His picture appeared on the covers of such magazines as

Newsweek and *Time. Sports Illustrated* named him "Athlete of the Year." People couldn't stop talking about this talented young star. Sports writers called it "Tigermania"—and it was just beginning. In the next two years, Tiger captured nine more tournament titles and took the number-one spot in the world rankings.

In 2000, Tiger set or tied 27 PGA Tour records. He won three **consecutive** major championships: the U.S. Open, the British Open, and the PGA Championship. He also won nine other tournaments that year. In a single season, Woods had earned more than $8 million in prize money. Other players said Tiger might turn out to be the greatest golfer who ever lived.

Children loved to watch him. So did their parents and grandparents. With his incredible talent and youthful

Tiger gets a kiss from a young fan in China.

personality, Woods attracted thousands of new fans to the game of golf.

How Golf Began

It's hard to say just when and how golf was invented. For hundreds of years, people have played similar games, using sticks to hit balls.

In 1744, Scottish players created the first written rules of golf. They used clubs made of wood and balls filled with

Golf began in Scotland on sandy, seaside courses called links.

boiled goose feathers. Players competed in sandy fields near the ocean called "links." Scottish golfers formed the Royal and Ancient Golf Club of St. Andrews and held some of the first true golf tournaments.

This type of golf spread quickly to England and nearby countries. Over the years, play-ers made improvements in the rules and equipment. In 1888, a man named John Reid built the first golf course in the

United States. He ordered wooden clubs and rubber balls from Scotland and taught his friends how to play.

Six years later, the United States Golf Association was formed. The USGA reworked the official rules of golf and set up national competitions. In 1916, the top male golfers created the Professional Golfers Association of America (PGA). They put together a series of professional tournaments and competitions now known as the PGA Tour.

The Ladies Professional Golf Association (LPGA) was founded in 1949.

Golf has become one of the world's most popular sports. More than 25 million people play golf. The United States alone has more than fourteen thousand golf courses. People of all ages and fitness levels enjoy the game. **Recreational** golfers may play for fun and exercise. For professionals, however, golf is an intense and competitive sport.

Today, people of all ages enjoy golf.

The Rules

It may sound simple: hit the ball into the hole. As many golfers have discovered, it's not that easy. Golf can be a very challenging game. It takes a lot of skill and concentration.

A golf course has eighteen "holes." On each hole, a player tries to hit the ball from an

Players begin each hole by "teeing off" (left). They "drive" the ball into the air and down the fairway, trying to get the ball as close to the cup as possible. It usually takes several strokes to get the ball into the cup on the putting green (above).

area called the "tee" down a long **fairway** and into a "cup" on a grassy area called a "putting green." The cup may be anywhere from about 100 to 575 yards (91 to 526 meters) from the tee, so it usually takes several hits of the ball, or "strokes," to reach it. The goal is to get from the tee to the cup in as few strokes as possible.

Players must try to avoid hit-ting the ball into "hazards" — water ponds and sand bunkers placed throughout the fairways. Each stroke adds to the player's score.

Players complete a "round" of golf when they have hit the

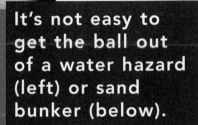

It's not easy to get the ball out of a water hazard (left) or sand bunker (below).

An overhead view
of a golf course

ball from the tee to the cup on
all eighteen holes. A tournament
may have two to four rounds,
taking place over several days.
At the end of a round or
tournament, the player with the
lowest score wins.

It takes the average golfer between three and five hours to complete a round. Recreational players may use golf carts to ride the course, but professionals must walk the entire length of

People who play for fun may use golf carts to travel from hole to hole (left). Professional golfers must walk the entire course (below).

the course. People called "caddies" carry the players' clubs.

Golfers usually play in foursomes (groups of four), though they may play in twosomes or by themselves. Single players compete against themselves, trying to beat their own previous score on the course.

Golf has a rather unusual way of keeping score. "Par" is the total number of shots it would take a professional golfer to complete a particular hole—usually three, four, or five shots. If a player gets the ball into the hole in one shot less than the par for that hole, he or she has hit a "birdie" on that hole. A score of two shots under par is called an "eagle."

Once in a great while, a player hits a perfect shot from the tee to the green. When that ball rolls right into the cup without another stroke, the

Golfers' reactions to
getting a birdie (left),
a hole in one (middle),
and a bogey (right)

player celebrates a "hole in one."
When a player hits one shot more
than (or "over") par, he or she has
"bogied." Two shots over par is a
"double bogey."

The Equipment

Golf is a game of tradition. The rules and **strategies** have stayed the same for a hundred years. The equipment, however, has improved greatly.

Golf balls are no longer made of goose feathers! A modern golf ball has a rubber core and a hard plastic shell. Dimples on

27

the outside of the shell make
the ball fly higher and farther
through the air. A standard golf
ball weighs about 1.5 ounces
(42.5 grams) and measures about
1.5 inches (3.8 centimeters)
around. Traditionally, the balls
used in competition are white.

Golfers don't play with wooden
clubs anymore. They use clubs

made of steel or **carbon fiber**. Every golf club has a handle covered by a soft grip. The length of the club is called the "shaft." A rounded "clubhead" sits at the bottom of the shaft. The front of the clubhead, called the "clubface," is the part that makes contact with the ball.

Golfers use different types of clubs for different types of shots. The clubs vary in length and in the weight, shape, size, and angle of the clubhead. A

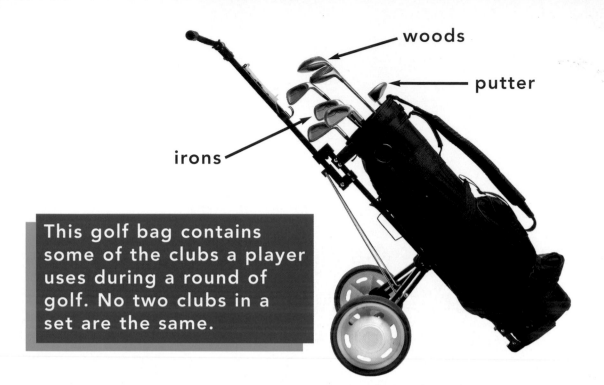

woods

putter

irons

This golf bag contains some of the clubs a player uses during a round of golf. No two clubs in a set are the same.

golfer may carry up to fourteen clubs—usually three or four "woods," nine or ten "irons," and a "putter."

Woods are used for the longest shots. Irons are used for shorter shots of varying distances.

The longest wood, called a driver, is used for teeing off (above). An iron called a chipping wedge is used for "chip shots"—high, short shots close to the green (right).

Usually, the longer the iron, the farther it will send the ball. As players get closer to the green, they tend to choose shorter irons.

A player uses a putter to roll the ball once it is on the green.

Putters are used mainly to roll the ball once it is on the green. A special golf bag keeps the clubs together in one place and makes them easier to carry.

Golfers wear spiked shoes that provide support. Some golfers play with a glove on one hand for extra comfort and grip.

Golf shoes (left) have spikes to help keep a player from slipping on the grass. Some players wear gloves for better grip (below).

On the Course

Golf is a game that encourages good manners and sportsmanship. Players carefully follow "course **etiquette**." For instance, after the first tee shot, the player farthest from the cup hits first. The others wait patiently for their turns. Players never stand or walk in

Golfers wait patiently and quietly while others are playing.

front of someone who is about to hit the ball. They try not to distract each other during play.

If a player hits a ball that looks as if it may hit another person on the course, the

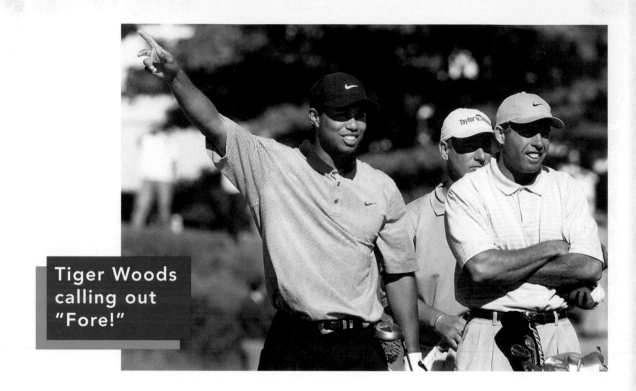

player quickly yells "Fore!" to warn the other person. Thoughtful players always replace their divots—the chunks of grass knocked loose by their clubs. As a courtesy to other players, they try to leave the course in even better condition than they found it.

The Golden Bear

Jack Nicklaus **dominated** men's professional golf for three decades. He won seventy professional tournament titles, including eighteen major championships—more than any other player in the world! Nicknamed the Golden Bear, Jack was 23 years old in 1963 when

Jack Nicklaus at the Masters in 1963

Nicklaus celebrating his 1986 Masters victory

he became the youngest player ever to win the Masters. That record stood for 17 years. In 1986, he became the oldest man to win the Masters, with an amazing come-from-behind victory at age 46.

Nicklaus at the British Open in 2000

The Professional Tour

There are many ways to play competitive golf. There are junior competitions for kids and community golf tournaments for adult amateur players. High-school and college teams compete with other schools in local, state, and national tournaments.

Teenage players looking at golf-course maps before a tournament

The best players in the world compete in international tour- naments on the professional men's and women's golf tours. These tours organize dozens of tournaments in countries all over the world.

Players travel from place to place to win titles, trophies, and prize money. For male players, the PGA Tour holds four major championships each year: the British Open, the U.S. Open, the PGA Championship, and the Masters. The LPGA Tour holds four major championships for women: The Kraft-Nabisco Championship, the U.S. Women's Open, the LPGA Championship, and the Women's British Open.

ROLEX ROLEX

THE OPEN CHAMPIONSHIP

UNISYS

ROYAL LYTHAM
& ST ANNES 2001
www.opengolf.com

HOLE	PAR	PLAYER	SCORE		
72	-10	DUVAL	★ 274		
72	-7	FASTH	277		
72	-6	WOOSNAM	278	POSITION AFTER 71 HOLES	SCORE FOR ROUND
72	-6	CLARKE	278		
72	-6	JIMENEZ	278		
72	-6	MAYFAIR	278		
72	-6	ELS	278		
72	-6	LANGER	278		

PLAYER
WELL DONE
DAVID
SEE YOU
AT
MUIRFIELD
2002

The British Open is one of the four major PGA championships (left). Australian golf great Karrie Webb is shown here playing in an LPGA Championship (below).

Tiger Woods was the first man to win all four Grand Slam events in a row—(from left to right) the 2000 U.S. Open, the 2000 British Open, the 2000 PGA Championship, and the 2001 Masters.

These tournaments are often called "Grand Slam" events because if a player were to win all four of these important tournaments in the same year, it would be called winning a "Grand Slam."

Sometimes a player is said to have won a "career Grand Slam." This means he or she has won each of the major championships at some point in his or her career, though not in the same year.

Juli Inkster celebrates her win at the 1999 LPGA Championship. That victory earned her a career Grand Slam.

To Find Out More

Here are some additional resources to help you learn more about the game of golf:

 **Books**

Curtis, Bruce, and Jay Morelli. **Beginning Golf.** Sterling Publishing Company, Inc., 2000.

Hayes, Larry, with Rhonda Glenn. **The Junior Golf Book.** St. Martin's Press, 1994.

Hull, Mary. **The Composite Guide to Golf.** Chelsea House Publishers, 1998.

Italia, Bob. **100 Unforgettable Moments in Pro Golf.** ABDO & Daughters Publishing, 1997.

Jensen, Julie. **Beginning Golf.** Lerner Publications Company, 1995.

Organizations and Online Sites

American Junior Golf Association

1980 Sports Club Drive
Braselton, GA 30517
http://www.ajga.com

The AJGA is a nonprofit organization dedicated to the growth and development of young men and women through competitive junior golf.

Ladies' Professional Golf Association

100 International Golf Drive
Daytona Beach, FL 32124
http://www.lpga.com

This is the official website of the professional women's golf tour.

Professional Golfers Association

112 PGA TOUR Boulevard
Ponte Vedra Beach, FL 32082
http://www.pgatour.com

This is the official website of the professional men's golf tour.

United States Golf Association

One Liberty Corner Road
Far Hills, NJ 07931
http://www.usga.org

The USGA is the governing body of amateur and professional golf in the United States.

Important Words

carbon fiber strong, lightweight material used to make some golf clubs

celebrity famous person

consecutive one after another

dominated was the best or most powerful of a group

etiquette rules of polite behavior

fairway grassy area used for play between the tee and the green

recreational referring to something done for the fun of it

strategies plans to achieve a goal

tournament series of games in which people or teams compete to win a championship

Index

Meet the Author

Christin Ditchfield is the author of more than twenty books for children, including nine True Books on sports. A former elementary-school teacher, she is now a freelance writer, conference speaker, and host of the nationally syndicated radio program *Take It To Heart!* Ms. Ditchfield makes her home in Sarasota, Florida.